QUEEN BEES, DRAMA QUEENS and CLIQUEY TEENS

Teen Life Confidential

HOW TO SURVIVE the FRIENDSHIP GAME

Anita Naik

About the Author

Anita Naik is an author, columnist, blogger and journalist. She started her career as advice columnist on the teen magazine *Just 17*, and is now the agony aunt at *Teen Now* magazine and *Avon Connects*. She is also a regular contributor to the parenting technology site Quibly (http://www.quib.ly) and writes regularly on the subjects of teens, tech, parenting, education and social media, across various media platforms and magazines. Anita is also the author of over 45 non-fiction books. For more information visit www.anitanaik.co.uk or Twitter @AnitaNaik.

With thanks to consultant Claude Knights at Kidscape for her advice in creating this title. Kidscape is committed to keeping children safe from abuse and bullying. The charity strives to equip children and young people with practical life skills, and with the knowledge and strategies to protect themselves from harm.

First published by Wayland in 2014
Copyright © Wayland 2014

Wayland
Hachette Children's Books
338 Euston Road
London NW1 3BH

Commissioning Editor: Debbie Foy
Editor: Annabel Stones
Illustrations: Harry Venning
Cover design by Lisa Peacock

A cataloguing record for this title is available from the British Library.

ISBN: 978 0 7502 8032 7
eBook ISBN: 978 0 7502 8034 1
Dewey: 302.3'4'08352-dc23
10 9 8 7 6 5 4 3 2 1

Printed in Great Britain

Wayland is a division of Hachette Children's Books, an Hachette UK company
www.hachette.co.uk

Contents

Introduction

'Girls are mean' and the queen bees, drama queens, and cliquey teens are just 'girls being girls'.
This is a refrain that girls (and their parents) hear from reception class, never mind Year 6 and beyond. It's almost as if being bossy/mean/spiteful/cruel and hurting friends is in our girl genes so we should all just stop complaining about it and get on with it, right?

Wrong! While girls do exclude, act meanly and divide and conquer, being mean and cruel isn't an essential girl trait that all 'friends' either have to act out or be a victim of. Being horrible to each other is not just 'girls being girls'. Mean behaviour (as you know if you've ever suffered from it) is a dangerous and powerful thing. It's painful, hurtful, confidence sapping and misery inducing. It makes you feel small, it makes you question your very being and if you don't deal with it, you can carry it with you for a lifetime.

Just look at the statistics: 87% of friends have bullied another friend, and girls who are treated badly by friends at the age of six have less of a chance of escaping bullies at the age of 11. That's two good reasons why this kind of girl behaviour has an official name and description: **'relational or social aggression'** (for more see page 40).

4

This is where one girl manipulates other girls to socially exclude someone from the group, spreads nasty rumours, betrays a person's trust and gets others to dislike her. It may include talking nastily about others, using code names to talk about friends, low-scale to high-scale ignoring and a range of other mean-style behaviours (nasty notes, hurtful messages, hiding personal property and using stares and bad looks to intimidate and so on).

Mixed in with this is a new cruelty spurred on by the latest technologies. The sheer range of devices and social and digital media has enabled some girls to become even more creative and inventive with their gossip and spite, offering a faster and more destructive (and often anonymous) way to torment and torture each other.

The good news is, negative girl friendships are not something you have to put up with and/or indulge in yourself. There are ways to combat and stop the tricks and slurs that can ruin your life, and also ways to identify where you are on that fine line between teasing and tormenting, and harmless and harmful behaviour.

If you're tired of all the dirty tricks, ridiculous dramas and the queen bees who try to inflict their toxic friendship on everyone, then this is the book for you.

Don't despair, because no matter how powerful these girls seem right now, you can deal with them. Follow the tips in this book and you'll not only feel stronger but you'll also move on to happier and kinder friendships for life.

CHAPTER ONE

Being popular

"Everyone wants to be popular. They are lying if they say they don't. Some girls like me are just popular. Maybe it's because we're nicer and more fun. I don't know. Anyway it's not my fault."

JADE, 13

"You have to be so fake if you want the popular girls to like you. At our school you have to pretend you like the music they like, wear the clothes they wear and talk to the boys they think are the best. If you don't they call you a geek or worse."

SAM, 12

The friendship game is a tricky one, **both hugely rewarding and all-encompassing, but also potentially upsetting and stressful.** It can feel like a constant battle where the goal posts of what's acceptable and what's not are constantly moving. The need to be popular and liked by others starts young, sometimes even in nursery where one girl might rule, and others follow. The problem is that these struggles get more dramatic, more important and more complicated as we get older.

We all want to be liked and to have lots of friends — partly because being popular feels like a sign to the world and ourselves that we are somehow worthy and that's why people like us. However, in a quest to be popular we can find ourselves doing all kinds of things that go against our better nature. Like pretending to be something we're not, or letting others dictate how we behave/dress/speak and even squashing our true self so that we fit into what we think others want.

At the root of this is the fact that being popular at school is not about who is the nicest and best kind of friend. It's often about how we dress, how we act, what we say and what we like. Sometimes it's down to who has the strongest personality, who is the prettiest or who is the toughest. It can even be about something else entirely. Inevitably at the top of this popularity pile are the girls who rule. The ones who get to decide who is in and who is out, and the ones who get the most attention.

Even if you're not friends with these girls, it's likely that they affect your life because what they do affects the lives of everyone around you. It's the reason why you need to learn how to deal with them and how to avoid their tactics and even how not to turn into one of them.

Quiz How far would you go to be popular?

1 *A popular girl at your school says she hates a band you secretly love. How do you respond?*

- **a** You agree, but feel like you're betraying them
- **b** You tell her all the reasons why she's wrong
- **c** You agree and find you are going off them

2 *Three girls you know tell you a rumour about a friend and ask you to pass it on. What do you do?*

- **a** Listen but don't pass it on
- **b** Tell your friend what's happening
- **c** Pass it on even though you feel bad

3 *Fashion-wise you dress to...*

- **a** Keep up with the trends at school
- **b** Please yourself
- **c** Fit in with your friends' looks

4 *You really like a boy at your school, but everyone calls him a nerd. Does it...*

- **a** Make you keep your feelings quiet?
- **b** Make you like him even more?
- **c** Put you off him?

5 *The most popular girl at school asks you to sit with her at lunch. How does it make you feel?*

- **a** Uneasy – you wonder what she wants from you
- **b** Uncomfortable – you have nothing in common
- **c** Happy – you really want to be friends with her

Mostly As You're one torn girl, stuck halfway between what you know is right and what you have to do to be popular. In many ways you toe the line perfectly even though you sometimes hate yourself for it. Perhaps you wish you could be a bit braver and stick up for what you believe in and know is right, but don't give yourself such a hard time. It's difficult to make a stand in the face of others.

Mostly Bs You're a girl who knows her own mind. Aside from making you a force to be reckoned with, we wouldn't be surprised if you were popular in your own right and for all the right reasons. You don't bow to others' opinions, or do the nasty for them. You know who you are and what you believe, and you stick firmly to it. Good for you.

Mostly Cs Like many girls, you would love to be in with the popular set. This doesn't make you a bad person but it's worth remembering that you need to be true to yourself on some level. This means not doing things that go against your gut instinct or make you feel sick afterwards. Plus even if you're in with the popular set you don't have to be a mirror image of them. Be yourself and you're more likely to find friends who like you for the real you.

The need to be popular

"Sometimes I think it would be nice to be popular and to have someone want to sit next to me for a change. Or to not make a face when they're asked to work with me. Even to have people to want to talk to me at break."

LILY, 14

The truth is we all have this need to fit in and be popular. We may not all want to be the queen bee but we all want to feel that we're liked and have friends. It's this reason that drives most of us to sometimes be something we're not, to keep quiet when we should speak up and to put up with things we've always said we wouldn't stand for.

If you feel the need to be popular and accepted all the time, the chances are you got this message when you were little from your parents. On a subconscious level, many parents push kids to have as many friends as possible, worrying that their children might be lonely or alone if they don't have lots of friends. If this rings true for you, it can make you think that you're letting your parents (or yourself) down if you can't make people like you. Or that you're not good enough if people don't like you.

On another level, you may feel that you have to be popular because that's

what girls do, even though you're essentially the kind of person who likes being by herself (there are more people like this than you might think).

Wherever you are on the popularity spectrum, what you need to realize is that there are positives and negatives to being popular and well-liked.

Positives to being popular:

* *People respect and like you.*

* *Your opinion counts.*

* *You feel good about yourself.*

* *You always have friends about.*

* *You rarely feel lonely.*

* *You get invited everywhere.*

Negatives to being popular:

* *You have to maintain your position.*

* *Everyone is always watching what you do.*

* *People expect a lot from you.*

* *It's stressful to have to maintain your popularity.*

* *It's tempting to get people to do what you want.*

* *You sometimes feel people don't know the real you.*

In terms of confidence, what is important to remember is not how many people like you, but how you feel about yourself inside. If your view of yourself relies on how many people tell you you're nice/pretty/clever/popular then your confidence levels are always at their mercy. This means that you're more likely to do what others ask, be a follower, be in a clique and even be a not very nice queen bee – just to feel good about yourself.

The key to being popular and happy with it is to:

* *Be as true to yourself as you can be.*

* *Like who you want to like.*

* *Dress the way you want.*

* *Be who you are.*

* *Not feel you have to conform to be liked.*

It's a very tall order (even as an adult) and yes, you may not rule the school world (and really there's not a lot of fun in that as you'll see later in the book) but the truth is you'll end up having strong friendships with people who like you for all the right reasons.

What affects our friendship behaviour?

"Are girls born to be mean? It seems like it. The mean girls at school are the same ones that were mean in junior school."

ELLIE, 12

Are we all born to behave the way we do? Is being mean, or popular, or funny, or manipulative an essential part of our personalities that we can't change? Thankfully not! All behaviour is something that is learnt — we get it from our parents, from what we watch and read, from the people we hang out with and from our role models. This can be good or bad depending on what you are modelling and who you are trying to be both knowingly and unknowingly. Here's what affects how we behave as friends.

The media

"Girls are always being mean to each other. I see it in movies and on TV. It's just the way we are."

EVIE, 11

Whether you realize it or not, what you watch, read and listen to plays a big role in influencing your view of friendships and how you behave with friends. Studies have found that popular TV shows where girls are gossipy, nasty to each other, back-stabbing and mean, directly influence how girls behave to each other in the real world and affect what they feel is acceptable and unacceptable.

13

Websites that deal in bitchy gossip about celebrities also make us feel that it's okay to be mean to someone just for the sake of it. Reality shows where we laugh at others or judge people's talents harshly all play a part in how we believe we can behave towards others.

This is not surprising when you think about it – after all, we are all influenced by the media around us. What's important is to think about what you're seeing and consider (1) if that really is the right way to behave or not and (2) why you're being drawn to this show/person. Below are some of the popular portrayals of friendships that you may come across in the media and translate into real life.

THE QUEEN BEE In nearly every teen show, book and film there is a queen bee. The mean and most popular girl around who rules. She's usually pretty, and has a pack of followers hanging on her every word and doing her every wish. 99% of the time she gets her comeuppance and sees the error of her ways (not always true in real life).

THE DRAMA QUEEN This is the girl who always happens to have the worst-case scenario going on. She's slightly hysterical about everything from friendships to a boy she likes and more.

THE POPULAR GIRL WHO HAS EVERYTHING This girl has the looks, the money, the boys and the clever brain. Teachers love her, boys love her – in fact, everyone loves her. She might be the nicest person in the world (or not) but she's also guaranteed to make you feel unworthy.

THE FRIGHTENING FRIEND This is the 'bad' girl. She's trouble and someone who doesn't do what the majority do. In shows and films and even in real life, people are drawn to her out of fear and because she can be fun.

THE GOSSIP GIRL This is the girl who has files on everyone. She knows who fancies who, who did what with whom, who is cheating and who is spreading the rumours. She seems harmless but really she's a troublemaker.

Your parents

"My mum is always falling out with her best friend. There's always a drama going on there."

TARA, 13

As we've said before, parents play quite a big role in determining how you choose friends and behave with them. This is because whether you pay attention to your parents or not, you can't help but be influenced by them. It's the reason why experts recommend that parents try to be good role models for social behaviour and friendships so that you can learn positive lessons from them.

Unfortunately, if your parents model negative friendship behaviours, such as gossiping and fighting with friends, then it tells you that this is normal and fine to replicate with your own friends.

Likewise if you see them in power struggles and being bossed about by friends, you're likely to copy this.

How your family expects you to behave is another factor in friendship behaviour. Many girls are brought up with the idea that they should be nice, quiet and accommodating. Such expectations often mean that you have to push everything negative that you feel, especially anger and defiance, out of sight. This creates girls who feel they have to be one thing on the surface and something else underneath. It's this that can turn you into a follower or a queen bee, or someone who doesn't feel she can express what she feels to others.

Role models

 "X is my role model. She's pretty and talented and doesn't seem to care about anyone but herself and that's pretty cool. She has friends who follow her and boys who just want to be with her and she's not nice to anyone. It's kind of funny."

EMMA, 12

There's a lot to be said about having a role model. They can inspire you, pick you up when you're down and help you find a way through some of the more tricky parts of being a teen. However, role models tend to be people you don't know, such as celebrities, actors and pop-stars. People who you only get a media view of, and this can be dangerous. While studies show that modelling the behaviour, thoughts and attitudes of successful people can help you become more successful, it can go wrong if you pick the wrong kind of role model.

For instance, if your role model is someone who is famous for treating others badly or puts up with bad behaviour from others, it can reinforce your own view of what is and isn't acceptable in relationships and friendships. It's one reason why real people are better role models as you can see them, warts and all, and get a clearer picture of why you respect and admire them.

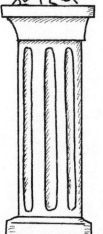

On the other hand, lots of people actively seek out role models who break the rules. This can be a good thing if it inspires you to work harder at something or ignore the people who bring you down. But beware! Role models (and these can be queen bee and drama queen friends) who 'suggest' that you should be hard, mean and horrible to others in order to be special aren't models to follow and be inspired by.

How you feel about yourself

"Being friends with Anna makes me feel popular. I worry that she'll dump me one day and then people will see that I am not as pretty or smart or worth knowing. That's why I stick with her when she's not being nice."
KARLY, 13

Your **self-esteem** (how you feel about yourself) also affects your friendship behaviours. If you're someone who likes who you are and are confident about yourself, then you're more likely to be friends with people for the right reasons. If you feel unworthy, unlikeable, or even not good enough, then you can end up being friends with people for a variety of bad reasons.

For example, you can attach yourself to a popular queen bee (and do what she says) so that others think you're as good as her, or be a doormat to a drama queen because you feel she needs you and that makes you feel worthy. You can also become part of a clique so that you feel protected and part of something, even if that clique goes against what you believe in.

Low self-esteem in friendships also leads you to avoid confrontation, act clingy and keep quiet about what you want, all of which is bad news even if you have a good friend. The good news is, there are ways to boost your self-esteem (see 8 ways to empower yourself on page 88 for more on this). Remember that although it takes time, you can do it.

High-self-esteem friendships have the following qualities:

* *The friendship is based on mutual liking and respect.*

* *Competition is low.*

* *Your time together is more positive than negative.*

* *Disagreements don't put the friendship in jeopardy.*

Low self-esteem friendships have the following qualities:

* *Part of you worries constantly that your friend will ditch you.*

* *You feel afraid to go against her in case she stops being your friend.*

* *She makes you feel guilty and sad more than happy.*

* *There are strict rules to your friendship that you can't break.*

Who are you friends with right now?

"Sometimes we're best friends, some days we're not. Sometimes she's funny and nice to be with, other times she's so horrible to me it hurts."

ELLA ON HER BEST FRIEND KATIE, BOTH 13

So what are your friends like? Are they people you turn to when you're in need, or need a laugh? Are they supportive, kind, helpful and truthful? Are they people you'd want to be trapped on a desert island with? Or somehow do they always leave you feeling bad? As if you have done something wrong or aren't quite good enough for them? Worse, do they do bad things that make you feel hurt, upset and miserable? Or encourage you to do mean things to others that make you feel bad? Or are they all of the above and more?

Don't worry if they are, because for most people that's what having friends can feel like! A minefield that seems to explode with every step you take. Sometimes it can get so bad that you feel as if it's just not worth having friends any more, but believe us when we say it is. The right friendships can bring real happiness and support you through the whole of your life. The trick is to weed out the bad from the good, and the destructive from the inspiring.

Real friends:

* *Listen to you.*

* *Tell the truth to you.*

* *Support you.*

* *Encourage you.*

* *Make you laugh.*

* *Are inclusive.*

* *Are fun to be with.*

* *Have your best interests at heart.*

* *Do good things for you for no reason.*

* *Let you be friends with others.*

Bad friends are:

* *Disloyal, spiteful and/or mean.*

* *Discouraging.*

* *Vindictive.*

* *Threatening.*

* *Hurtful.*

* *People who make you feel bad.*

* *People who have their own best interests at heart.*

* *More interested in themselves than you.*

CHAPTER TWO

The girls who rule school

"We're always friends at the start of the day but by lunch she's telling other friends to ignore me. I try to make up but she just walks off with other girls. After school she'll message me as if nothing has happened and then get huffy and stroppy when I don't respond. She's my best friend but then sometimes she's not."

EMILY, 11

In ten years' time, you're not going to remember the name of the boy you fancy or even the pair of jeans you so desperately want to buy right now, but you will remember the girls who were mean to you. They're the girl or girls who ruled your school, the ones who played dirty tricks, spread gossip, excluded people and had the power to make, shake or break your day.

Yes, we're talking queen bees, drama queens, gossip girls and the cliques and how they affect you, even when they're not directed at you. In an ideal world, those mean chicks would of course get their comeuppance. Just like in the movies they'd be caught out and made to change. However, revenge and karma are not worth getting hung up on because school isn't forever and they will be out of your life sooner than you think.

This is all well and good, but it does mean that until then you have to learn how to spot them, deal with them and of course avoid turning into one of them yourself.

So here's where it all starts. Ask yourself this:

* *What are you willing to put up with in the name of friendship – a bit of teasing, tormenting or a torrent of abuse?*

* *When push comes to shove, what kind of friend are you – a good one, a scared one or just a good-time one?*

* *Are you secretly channelling your inner mean streak or doing your best to avoid it?*

* *Are your friendship actions motivated by jealousy or wanting your friends to be happy? Or maybe a bit of both?*

As none of us are wholly good or bad, it can sometimes be hard to tell whether you are being a good friend or not. We all want to fit in, and often this means gossiping and enjoying a good laugh at someone else's expense, but the question is how far are you willing to go? What dirty tricks have you played or put up with in the name of friendship?

Quiz What kind of girl friend are you?

1 *You're out shopping when you see a friend holding hands with the most nerdy of guys. What are you most likely to do?*

- **a** Instant message your best friend about it
- **b** Go over to them and say hello
- **c** Take a picture and then post it on Facebook
- **d** Wait to see if she kisses him so you can tell everyone
- **e** Feel annoyed/upset that she didn't tell you she was seeing him first

2 *Your best friend has gained weight and asks you if she looks fat. You say...*

- **a** No of course not – then tell your other friends that she's gained weight
- **b** She's lovely just as she is
- **c** Yes, and slip in that everyone's talking about it
- **d** No, but drop hints that she shouldn't eat so much
- **e** Does she think you're fat?

3 *A girl you want to be friends with says she's dying to come to your party but won't if you invite X – a girl you really like. What do you do?*

- **a** Explain to X why you can't invite her
- **b** Invite X because you like her better
- **c** Feel flattered and drop X as a friend
- **d** Invite them both but make a big fuss of the popular girl to see what she knows about what's going on
- **e** Tell everyone what a massive dilemma this is and how much it's upset you

4 *No one talks to the new girl at school because rumour has it she steals other people's boyfriends. She asks to sit with you at lunch – what do you do?*

    a Say, 'Sorry I've just finished but here have the table'
    b Make friends with her
    c Say – 'Sorry this seat is taken'
    d Say yes and try and get some 'stories' out of her
    e Tell her this happened to you and ruined your life

5 *You spot a friend buying what looks like sexy underwear. Do you take advantage of what you've seen?*

    a Yes, you tell all your closest friends!
    b No, it's her private business
    c No, but you let her know you've seen her and then hold it against her
    d Yes, you send her an anonymous instant message
    e Yes, because she should be telling you these things

6 *There is a major falling out amongst your friends. Which person are you?*

    a The one who gets pulled into the argument
    b The one who tries to get everyone to be friends
    c The one who started the fight
    d The one who stirs it up and sees what happens
    e The one who is crying and wailing

Mostly As – Cliquey friend Your friendship tactic is to keep your head down and follow so that no one can pick on you or gossip about you. The only trouble is you're not being true to yourself.

25

You hate following and having to do what others want. While it's hard to be yourself (and risk being by yourself) when there are stronger personalities around, in the long run it's better than hiding your true self away.

Mostly Bs – Fabulous friend You're a fabulous friend – the kind who knows her own mind, and isn't afraid to say and do what she thinks, even if it means standing outside the friendship game. You're also someone who has integrity – that's great morals and standards. It makes you both an excellent friend and a force to be reckoned with amongst all the drama queens and mean girls.

Mostly Cs – Queen bee You are the girl in charge and the truth is you're a troublemaker amongst your friends. You like to be the girl in the know and the one who decides who is in and who is out. The problem is, you often don't care whose feelings get hurt in the process so beware – what goes around comes around. It may be time to change your queen bee ways!

Mostly Ds – Gossip girl You may not think you're being malicious, but stirring things up with salacious rumours worthy of a Hollywood blogger reflects pretty badly on you. You may not mean to be such a gossip girl (and probably don't realize you are) but your words hurt others and your gossip causes trouble so think before you speak, text and spread the word.

Mostly Es – Drama queen It's all about you. You can't bear the spotlight to be on others because then it means people aren't interested in your problems and woes. As a result, you tend to not notice what's happening to friends unless it directly affects you and your problems. It means you hold onto your support group – oops sorry friends – by making them feel that they can't leave your side. It's manipulation at its best, whether you realize it or not.

Profile of a drama queen

"Oh my god! That is just so horrible. Don't talk to me ever again. I can't believe you went to see the film without me. You knew how much that film meant to me. I can't believe you'd be so mean knowing what I'm going through."

FREYA, 13, DRAMA QUEEN

Demanding divas are hard work. Watch them in action on TV and they can seem glamorous, exciting and funny but in real life they are exhausting. As friends they demand a lot of time and energy and equal amounts of looking after. The problem is that they have to sweep you up into their personal melodramas. And they ALWAYS need you to help solve or witness some urgent drama (and with drama queens there is always a drama).

That, in a nutshell, is what's wrong with a friend who is a drama queen – you can't have a drama if there is no one to play to. Which means that in order for drama queens to feel fulfilled – YOU have to be there. To get you on their side they will use their dramas to appeal to your nice side, your helpful side and your sympathy.

If you refuse to be drawn in and play your part, they'll throw a tantrum of epic proportions (see Freya's quote above). In terms of friendship this can take its toll on you and your reputation at school. Aside from being tarred with the same diva brush, being friends with a drama queen can leave you feeling secondary and unworthy. What's more, constantly being around all the drama is wearing and not good for your own peace of mind.

Why then are so many of us drawn to being friends with people who love to be divas? Well let's be honest, tiring stuff aside, being best friends with a drama queen is also very entertaining, funny and can add a welcome splash of colour to life. On a good day they can be the life and soul of a party, cracking jokes in lessons, impersonating teachers and having fun. On down days their insatiable desire for attention will make you feel as if you have been through four spin cycles in a washing machine.

If you don't believe us, think of this. If you have a problem, it's likely it is never as big or as bad as what they're going through. If they do take your problem seriously, doesn't it still somehow end up being all about them? Plus, and this is the key point with drama queens, though they may seem weak and helpless, they are master manipulators. They know exactly how to control the people in their lives to get what they want, which is attention and more attention. It's not the best basis for friendship, is it?

You're a drama queen if:

* *You're not really that interested in anyone else's life.*

* *Everything that happens to you always feels like a big deal, even the small stuff.*

* *You don't feel people pay attention to you unless you have a drama going on.*

* *You thrive on drama.*

* *You hate other people's dramas.*

* *Your friends support you, rather than the other way round.*

You have a drama queen as a 'friend' if:

* *Your friendship is always about her.*

* *You walk on eggshells so as not to upset her.*

* *She doesn't really know any of the deep stuff about you.*

* *You feel you can't stop being friends with her as she needs you.*

* *You feel your issues aren't as important as hers.*

* *She regularly makes demands on you to change plans to be with her.*

Profile of a queen bee

"The queen bee popular girls are always the pretty, confident girls. They get away with everything they say and do because everyone wants to hang out with them and be known as one of their friends."

LILY, 13

We all know a queen bee – even in adult life.
She's the girl who is popular, powerful and has a posse of girls who follow her. She can control her friends, dominate classrooms and divide and rule way too easily. Adults are often fooled by her and she even manages to fool her followers for a while by pretending to be both nice and a friend to all. The reality is, queen bees need to be in charge and this

ultimately means that they don't react well to anyone who dares to go against what they want.

So what makes some girls so adept at being a queen bee? Experts say that it's all down to their background – that's the life lessons they have learnt so far. Queen bees believe they're entitled to have it all – whether it's the top position amongst friends, the hottest guy or the lead in the school play. If things are going their way, they can be nice and friendly (and a few queen bees are actually like this all the time). However, if things don't go their way, or you get something or someone they want, they are likely to take revenge with a whole range of dirty tricks.

Unfortunately, being particularly savvy with their social skills (another lesson learnt from their backgrounds) queen bees often get away with their dirty tricks because they are popular and so have people to back them and their tricks up. The very smart queen bees don't even do the dirty work themselves, but make their thoughts clear and get others to do the dirty for them.

So why are we so drawn to queen bees? Well because they are powerful and attractive (in various ways). Being with them can make us feel invincible and part of something wonderful (even if sometimes we doubt what we're doing). This kind of friendship can also make us feel as if we're the chosen ones who are lucky to be friends with someone so great. On the other hand, fear can also keep us at the queen bee's side. Fear that they'll be mean to us or play tricks on us, or even ostracize (exclude) us if we don't do what they want us to.

You're a queen bee if you use your popularity to:

* *Get attention.*
* *Get what you want.*
* *Gain respect.*
* *Manipulate situations to your advantage.*
* *Control your friends and others.*
* *Punish people you don't like.*

You have a queen bee as a friend if:

* *You never know where you stand with her.*
* *You feel afraid of her.*
* *You do things she wants, not what you want.*
* *She says things that hurt people.*
* *She does things that hurt people.*
* *She makes you feel as if you are lucky to be her friend.*

Profile of a cliquey teen

"My mum gets cross when I tell her what my best friends say. She's always saying, 'Why are you friends with these girls? Be your own person. Tell them they are being mean.' But she doesn't understand, they're my friends. They get me."

HANNAH, 12

A clique is a group of friends. Nothing wrong with that you may think, but a clique is essentially a closed, tight-knit group of friends who tend to not let anyone else in. This is great if you're in one, but not great for all the girls who are being excluded (and not so great for you if the clique turns against you).

It can be fun being part of a clique. It makes you feel special and connected to the girls around you, and that's why girls are drawn to them.

However, consider this: do you have a love-hate relationship with your friends? Do you adore them, love them and willingly follow them everywhere, but have you also been hurt, abandoned or betrayed by them? Or have you done that to others in your group just because they dared to stand out? If so, it's likely you're in a clique. And that is what's wrong with cliquey teens – one minute you love each other (and hate everyone else), and the next you're the person everyone loves to hate.

The biggest problem with cliques is that eventually familiarity does breed contempt and girls turn on each other. When that happens, all kinds of dirty tricks take place; rumours, gossip, exclusions, pretending to be friends and then spreading rumours, and more. This is why being a cliquey teen isn't always the safest thing to be. A clique that will do anything for you can also do anything to you.

You're in a clique if:

* *You love the fact that you're in an exclusive group.*

* *You actively don't let others in.*

* *You feel that you and your friends are better than others outside the clique (this can be for the way you dress, your interests, your look etc.).*

* *You don't socialize with anyone outside the group.*

* *There are 'rules' to being in your group that you all keep to.*

You have a friend in a clique if:

* *She chooses them over you.*

* *She won't go against what they say.*

* *She doesn't stick up for you if they're being mean.*

* *She doesn't know who she is without them.*

* *She is a copy of all the other girls.*

Girl gangs

There is a growing trend in some areas for girl gangs. These are friends who claim allegiance to each other in a much stronger way than cliques. These gangs have strict rules about what's acceptable and allowed, and there are often dire consequences for stepping out of line. The friendships here are based on power, intimidation, jealousies and more. If you're being pulled into a girl gang and are too scared to step away or are having problems with girls from a gang, it's vital to seek help ASAP (see Help Section on page 92).

Profile of a gossip girl

"I love gossip. Stuff about celebrities, magazines, Facebook and all the things you hear about everyone. Of course I pass it on, doesn't everyone?"

ZOE, 13

Hands up if you love *Gossip Girl*...! We're talking the book and TV show about an anonymous blogger who spreads rumour, intrigue and gossip to stir up trouble and cause major dramas. In essence that's what being a gossip girl is all about: being the person who is in charge of what's being said about others and what's being spilled. It may be less mean than the queen bee behaviour, but it's done so that you can feel at the heart of every drama going and be in control of all the information going around.

As a result, a friend who is a gossip girl is an interesting mix of drama queen and queen bee. It's a manipulative position that's the enemy of real friendship: confidences are betrayed, stories are exaggerated and trouble is caused all for the delight of one person.

Being friends with a gossip girl can of course be fun – after all, other people's dramas seem exciting – especially at school. Being in the know about what's going on can feel powerful and thrilling. However, aside from being tarred with the gossip brush (ie. no one will ever trust you or confide in you ever again), spreading gossip is both dangerous and malicious, and can ruin people's lives.

If you're a gossip girl it can be hard to change your ways. You need to remind yourself that a lot of gossip is made up and untrue. It's put out there by people who have an agenda to hurt and bully someone. You may not have made it up, but by spreading it you're part of the problem.

You're a gossip girl if:

* *You don't see a problem in spreading rumours.*

* *You really believe that no secret is a secret.*

* *You love to stir up trouble.*

* *You don't censor what you say about others.*

* *You love to exaggerate a drama for fun.*

* *You use social media and new tech to your advantage.*

You have a gossip girl as a friend if:

* *You can't trust her with any secret.*

* *Your whole friendship is based on talking about others.*

* *You hate that others don't trust you because of her.*

* *You feel obliged to tell her what's going on, knowing that she'll pass it on.*

* *Everyone distrusts her.*

CHAPTER THREE

The downside of friendships

"I don't understand it. We were best friends and then I went on holiday. When I came back she ignored me. She won't sit next to me. She won't talk to me and has gone off with another girl. I feel like I have done something wrong even though I know I haven't."

NINA, 12

There are a multitude of positives to having friends – from having a laugh to sharing secrets, having someone to hang out with and even someone to rely on when you're down. If you have good friends, then you know the power of friendships and how long lasting they can be. However, no matter how good you are at making friends, and no matter how many friends you have, friendships can be very tricky.

Sometimes a good friend can turn nasty, or you can fall out with a best friend and suddenly feel isolated and alone. Sometimes friends can play mean tricks or try to manipulate you to get what they want, or even say one thing to your face and another behind your back.

On the one hand this is all part of learning how to handle friendships and deciding what you should and shouldn't put up with. It teaches you who to trust, how to have resilience and even when to forgive.

Having said that there is a distinct downside to friendships that you have to learn to deal with. This downside is all about the mind games that friends play, the dirty tricks they do and the way some girls need to keep you down. It's friendship but not as we usually think of it, as it treads the fine line between being friends and being a bully.

Relational aggression and friendships

"The cliques at my school are so mean. They think they're better than everyone else. They laugh when I walk by or mimic my voice or give me dirty looks. It really hurts my feelings but when I say that they say, 'Oh can't you take a joke?'"

ANON, 11

Relational aggression is the name given to the above kind of behaviour. It's the use of friendship as a weapon and some girls quickly learn that they can gain power (and attention and respect) by excluding others. The way they do this is by forming close friendships in a closed circle, also known as a clique.

While social groups are common at school – we all gravitate towards girls who like the same things as us, whether it's fashion, music or sport – what makes these girl cliques and groups different are the following things:

* *One girl rules the group and has the power to influence the others' behaviour.*

* *The group is closed to outsiders.*

* *Friends in the group do everything together.*

* *Being yourself and being friends with others outside of the group is not accepted.*

* *There are strict rules to being in the group.*

* *The behaviour within the group is aggressive towards others, especially girls they are jealous of. Tactics include: gossiping, dirty looks, whispers and 'jokes'.*

Cliques and queen bees often rule by putting others down. They use their popularity and the fact that they are in a group to get what they want. As a result, they are the reason why so many people feel angst and conflict at school. If that rings a familiar bell, don't despair here's how to deal with them and not let them get you down.

Dealing with mind games

"It's the laughing that gets me down – every time I say something in class or walk past them, the laughing starts. It makes me feel self-conscious and like I'm some big joke to everyone."

MJ, 12

Psychological games are the behaviours that are done on purpose to play with your mind. The purpose of them is to keep you down, make you feel low, suggest that you're not good enough and hint to you that everyone else knows this. Why do they happen? Well sometimes because others are jealous of you, or because they have issues they can't deal with elsewhere (and so they take it out on you). Or sometimes it's because these people like the feeling of power it gives them.

On the whole, psychological games are the ones churned out by cliques and their ruling queen bees. This is because vicious emotional games can only be played with numerous players. The queen bee instructs her followers and they carry through with the game at hand. So what are these psychological games? Well whispering, sniggering, back-stabbing, mimicking and copying, back-handed compliments like, 'You're really great at that, but really rubbish at everything else' or constant laughing and nasty looks are all weapons that these girls use.

Basically it's anything belittling and intimidating to you, such as:

* *Taunts, threats, teasing and name-calling.*

* *Making faces and using sarcasm.*

* *Intentionally excluding someone from a group.*

* *Spreading rumours.*

* *Hiding your things and clothes.*

* *Getting others to join in with the intimidation.*

* *Making jokes at your expense.*

* *Using code names for you and sending nasty messages.*

One of the reasons why psychological games are difficult to deal with is that many of them are covert (hidden). Unlike a physical fight, the signs of emotional bullying and intimidation are invisible. What's more, many mean girls are clever at hiding their true selves from parents, adults and teachers and being nasty when no one in authority is looking. Games like these also have the effect of slowly belittling you, taking away your confidence and self-esteem and so making you feel as if (1) you can't deal with it and (2) you somehow deserve what's happening to you.

If you feel this way, the first thing to do is to remind yourself every time it happens that you have nothing to feel embarrassed or ashamed about. An emotional by-product of having psychological games like these played on you is to feel ashamed that it's happening, and it's often this that stops people from speaking up. Other times fear can stop you from speaking out and confronting the bullies. Fear that the behaviour will get worse if you say something, fear that people will hate you even more for speaking out and fear that no one will believe you.

The fact is, you don't have to ignore it or stand up to it face-to-face. The way to deal with psychological games is to be brave enough to tell someone what is going on. Try an older sibling, a teacher, a parent, a friend, or a bullying charity helpline (see Help section page 92). Talking about what's happening will do a number of things instantly:

* *It will help you to see that you're not alone.*

* *It will help you to feel in control of what's happening.*

* *It will reassure you that others can help change this situation.*

* *It will remind you that someone else is to blame here, not you.*

* *It will help you to see that you can overcome what's happening.*

Dealing with dirty tricks

"We used to be such good friends and tell each other everything. After I started going out with this boy, she told everyone we were having sex. It was a lie but it got round and then she denied saying it, even though I saw the text she sent about us. Now she's telling everyone I am bad mouthing her."

ELLIE, 13

Dirty tricks like the one Ellie's friend pulled above are done again and again. Most commonly, these tricks have betrayal as their basis and tend to come from 'friends' who you once told something private to, and who have now made the 'secret' common knowledge. Or 'friends' who have made up a lie about you in order to gain something in return. Perhaps the lie/rumour is about a boy you fancy, or something about your family, or your likes and dislikes or even a personality quirk. Dirty tricks can also be about backstabbing or even being one thing to your face and another behind your back.

Dirty tricks also include excluding and isolating people. Perhaps you're not invited to a party and everyone else is, or everyone sits together at lunch and ensures there's no space for you, or no one picks you for teams at school.

Exclusion and isolation are not only done between 'friends' trying to make a point, but are also two of the top tricks that queen bees use to control their followers. The message being, 'toe the line and do as I say or you'll be excluded and find yourself alone.'

Where psychological games are about power and gaining control, dirty tricks can be about anything from getting revenge or expressing jealousy to trying to be popular or simply getting one over you. The way to deal with dirty tricks is confrontation. Tell the friend face-to-face that what she is saying/doing is mean and that you know what she's up to (think about what she's gaining from playing this dirty trick). Often the friend in question won't be a good friend, but a friend who is used to getting her way or feels that you are moving away from her.

If you can't bring yourself to confront her, your next best bet is to ignore her. Dirty tricks tend to fade away if you ignore what's happening (unless the rumour/lie/truth is destructive in which case see the advice for dealing with psychological games). If you suspect a friend is playing a series of dirty tricks on you, the best thing to do is back away and don't give her any part of you. A person can't play tricks on you if you refuse to be a part of it.

Crafty tricks

*"She told everyone I was cheating in my exams
and the next thing I was up in front of my teacher.
I cleared stuff up and she said it was all a joke
but it wasn't funny."*

JACQUI, 12

**Crafty, or insidious, tricks are gradual tricks that
become harmful.** For example, a friend drip-feeding
the idea to others that you can't be trusted, that you're a
gossip or flirt, or that you steal other people's boyfriends.
Sometimes these tricks start off as a joke but the ideas
quickly spread and suddenly you can find yourself with
a nasty reputation or the feeling that others are talking
about you all the time.

Crafty tricks are:

* *Spreading gossip.*

* *Spreading rumours.*

* *Making up lies.*

* *Telling half truths.*

The thing with crafty tricks is that sometimes there is no
malice behind them. They are the result of gossip girls
who like to spread rumours and suggest things just to up
their own status, or a joke that's got seriously out of hand.
Other times they are malicious and done to turn everyone
against you. The solution is to go to the root of the
problem and find the reason for the initial trick. Asking a

47

friend to clear it up is one way of dealing with this, another is to make it clear to everyone you know that it is a lie.

If the trick is a joke, don't be fooled by the lines, 'Can't you take a joke?' Or, 'Where's your sense of humour?' These are get-out clauses for people who don't want to take responsibility for their actions. A joke is only a joke if both sides enjoy the banter. Real friends will stop and apologize if you tell them their joke isn't funny or is hurting you. Bad friends will try to make it all about you and then use it against you!

Finally be aware of your own behaviour. If you're a friend of a gossip girl, it's likely that you also indulge in spreading a little gossip. Sometimes being on the other side of it is a good glimpse into why these tricks are so painful and should be avoided.

Dealing with drama queens

"SJ texts me constantly. There is always a drama, always something awful happening. It's exhausting to be her friend."

JULES, 13

As we said in Chapter 2, drama queens are entertaining and colourful. They make us feel wanted and needed, but the reality is there is a distinct downside to being friends with them. For starters, they use their petty dramas to get attention and to control you and your life. Then, having a friend who is a drama queen is exhausting because this person reacts to everything with OTT emotion and behaves in a variety of attention-seeking ways – think crying, illness, hysteria and drama, drama, drama.

If you're unsure if your friend is a drama queen or not, ponder this:

* *Does your friend spend all your time together talking about her life?*

* *Does she obsess about her small and petty dramas all the time?*

* *Does she say she needs your support/help/advice all the time to make it through the day?*

* *Does she turn on you for minor things she's blown out of proportion, such as you talking to someone else at lunch?*

* *Does she make you feel guilty or punish you if you're not there for her?*

* *Do you often feel angry that so much of your time is about her stuff?*

All these emotions are common when you're friends with a drama queen, because drama queens appeal to your sympathy and better nature to help satisfy their demands. Don't be fooled by her manipulations or the way she tries to make you feel bad. Drama queens are not weak and helpless or needy but friendship manipulators who use others to satisfy their needs.

The best way to deal with a friend who is a drama queen is to set clear boundaries. This means time limits on how long you discuss for things and when. It also means bringing yourself into the conversation more often (remember if there's no space for you, then this isn't a friendship) and not allowing her to attack or admonish you when you don't want to talk about her all of the time. Most of all, for the sake of your self-esteem and your emotions, you need to spread your friendship wings and branch out, otherwise you'll always be just a side actor to the drama queen's starring role.

Tech tricks: social networking pitfalls and text wars

"Someone is posting mean stuff about me on a social networking site. It's one of those anonymous sites where you don't have to put your name so I don't know who's saying it but everyone can see it. It's driving me crazy as I get alerts all night and it's making me look at everyone I know and wonder if they're really my friends."

ALI, 13

Texting, smartphones, YouTube, direct messaging, email and social networking, such as Facebook, are all brilliant ways to stay in touch with your friends. Aside from sharing pictures, humour and gossip they are brilliant ways to forge deeper friendships and stay in touch 24/7. The downside is, of course, these things are yet another way for all the people playing psychological games and dirty tricks to get to you.

What's worse, because they're happening in the virtual world there is no relief from them. They can come at you all day and night, at home and on holiday and they can spread faster than a cold.

You're being harassed online if someone is:

* *Texting threatening or nasty messages to you.*

* *Posting an embarrassing or humiliating video of you on YouTube.*

51

* *Instant messaging you nasty comments.*

* *Setting up fake profiles online to make fun of you.*

* *Spreading rumours and pictures of you online.*

Thankfully there are many ways you can deal with being attacked via social networking sites and through text wars. Firstly, keep everything you are sent so that you have evidence of what's happening (especially if it's threatening as you may want to involve the police later).

Secondly, do not respond and if you are being sent a barrage of nastiness, switch off your tech. Nothing will stop cyberbullying faster than closing down your networking page, coming off sites and changing your mobile number (and then limiting who you give your new number to). Yes, it's drastic stuff but don't underestimate the effect that cyberbullying can have on your mental health.

The other way to deal with it is to report online bullying to the Internet Service Provider (ISP) or social networking site (Facebook has protocols for this, see Help section page 92). If it's happening via your phone, report it to your mobile phone provider. Also block instant messages, emails and people on social networking sites who send you upsetting things or post upsetting things about you.

Bear in mind that all kinds of dirty tricks can happen online that may not feel like bullying but they are. For instance:

* *Friends who chat to each other and exclude you/ ignore you online.*

* *Friends who post embarrassing pictures of you online and tag all your other friends.*

* *Friends who spread gossip about you online.*

* *Friends who post horrible pictures and stories on your timeline or to your email or text.*

* *Friends who IM you hateful things.*

Friends who are trouble

"H is a great friend but she loves to do stuff that gets us into trouble. I don't think she means to but she just gets an idea and makes it look like fun even though I know it won't be."

ANON, 13

We all have friends who are trouble. The ones who love a bit of danger and breaking the rules! On the whole it's up to them what they do, but the only problem is they will inevitably drag you into their schemes too. This is because friends who are trouble are also the ones who tend to have strong personalities that enable them to manipulate you to go against your better judgment. So they can cleverly suggest that you break curfews, or skip school, or try dangerous substances. Others may entice you to break the law and say shoplift — tempting and teasing you with the idea that it will be fun and 'everyone does it.'

In our hearts, we all know the friends who are trouble. **The trick is to stand up to them and assert your view**. In good friendships this isn't a problem and you'll find many friends will respect what you say, even if they disagree with you. However, in some cases saying no to friends who are trouble can be hard. They might get angry or vindictive, or threatening and scary. Which is why it pays to think about (1) your friendships and (2) how to deal with them.

Remember 'each to their own' – which means if they are adrenaline junkies who love doing things for thrills that's up to them. It's only a problem if they insist that you do it too. In which case keep telling yourself that you do not have to do the things they suggest. If they won't leave you alone or become threatening, then this is the time to speak to someone who can help. Talking about how to handle tricky friends like this is something we all have to do at some stage in life, and even though it's hard it can be done.

Friends who are trouble:

* *Will always seek out the next big thrill.*

* *Always want company as it's boring doing it alone.*

* *Tend to get aggressive if their ideas are rejected.*

* *Have a reason why they are seeking out trouble (whether they know it or not).*

* *Often don't mean to be bad friends but don't know how to be good ones.*

Troubled friends

"Lee has a really bad family life. I feel for her and try to help her but I worry about her when she's home and not at school. She won't let me tell anyone what's happening there."

SAM, 13

Troubled friends are friends with problems. Maybe that's problems with other friends at school, problems at home, problems with bullying or bigger problems to do with health, feeling depressed and more. The issue here is that it's easy to start feeling responsible for friends with problems, and while caring and wanting to help is part of being friends, you shouldn't feel that their problems are your responsibility.

The best way to help troubled friends is to encourage them to seek help, from someone who can really help such as a parent, teacher, a helpline or someone that you both trust. Suggest that you go with them when they seek help or that you ask on their behalf, but whatever you do don't keep big secrets that shouldn't be kept.

If you're at all worried, anxious or afraid for a friend's safety or health, or even their general well-being, to the point that you're scared, tell someone what is happening. Start with your own parents and let them direct you towards what to do next. Remember, while friendship is about keeping confidences, sometimes friends tell things to friends that they don't have the courage to tell the people who can really help. In these instances, you're being a good friend to step in and help them sort it out.

CHAPTER FOUR

What kind of friend are you?

"I think I'm a good friend. I care about my friends, I try not to boss them about but at the same time I am no pushover. I like them to agree with me and do what I do otherwise why be friends with someone?"

LAUREN, 14

So far we've talked about friendships and the types of friends you may encounter along the way. **The big question is, however, what kind of friend are you?** Where do you fit in on the scale from queen bee to gossip girl? Are you part of a clique or group? Are you a leader or a follower? Or an outsider who doesn't want to get involved? Do you put up with mean behaviour or are you an unwilling/willing member of the dirty tricks brigade?

It's important to know what kind of friend you are for a number of reasons. Firstly the kind of friend you are directly affects how you feel about yourself, and also how others view you. This in turn affects your confidence levels and your self-esteem.

Plus sometimes it can be an eye-opener to discover that you are actually not the kind of friend you thought you were. Your first step in working out what kind of friend you are is to think about what kind of people you are friends with.

Consider these questions:

* *How have you chosen your current friends?*

* *Are they people you have something in common with?*

* *Have you fallen together because one friend has made you her friend?*

* *Do you like being with your friends (it may sound silly but lots of people don't)?*

* *If you had to make friends all over again what would you do differently?*

* *Do your friends make you happy or sad?*

* *How proactive are you in making friends?*

Thinking about your current circle of friends can give you a real insight into the kind of person you are. For instance, if you have nothing in common with your friends and you have all been brought together by a central friend, it's likely that this friend dominates the group. If you feel you'd do things completely differently if you had to start again, it's likely you don't really like who you are when you're with your current friends and need a change. If your friends make you sad and/or you can't even remember why you are friends, it's time to move on.

Quiz **What's your friendship style?**

1 *A friend has had a terrible unflattering haircut. She asks for your opinion. What do you do?*

    a Change the subject – it's best not to get involved
    b Reassure her, saying, 'You're lovely just as you are'
    c You're honest – after all, she wants your opinion

2 *Your friends are making fun of a guy you secretly fancy. What do you do?*

    a Walk away so he doesn't think you're part of it
    b Join in – you don't want them to know the truth
    c Tell them to 'shut up' – after all, what do they know?

3 *You're great at all the geeky subjects. Do your friends know?*

    a No, it's none of their business
    b No, you always play it down
    c Yes, you rub it in their faces

4 *Are you the kind of girl…*

    a Everyone is wary of?
    b Everyone likes?
    c Everyone wants to be friends with?

5 *A friend is in trouble – how do you help?*

    a By giving her space and not crowding her
    b By telling everyone she needs support because X has happened
    c With tough love – you just have to get on with things

6 *Your best friend falls out with the school queen bee, what worries you about it?*

   a That you'll have to take sides
   b That you'll be tarred with the same brush
   c Nothing – you aren't afraid of anyone

7 *Your friendship style is...*

   a Be friends but don't get too involved
   b Give everything and hope people like you
   c Be strong so that people respect you

8 *A group of girls shut you out. How do you feel?*

   a You don't care
   b Upset and rejected
   c Furious

9 *If someone had to describe your best traits, they'd say...*

   a Independent and laid back
   b Caring and considerate
   c Strong and powerful

10 *You hear some bad gossip about yourself. How do you respond?*

   a You pretend you don't care
   b You cry, get upset and tell everyone
   c You get angry and find the culprit

Mostly As – The outsider friend/Isolated friend

Your friendship style is to stay out of things completely whether it's drama, trouble, gossip or fights. On the one hand this is great because it means you rarely come into conflict with anyone, but on the other it means you never really connect with anyone. For a friendship to deepen, some level of involvement has to happen. This means sticking up for friends when they need you, or getting angry when someone you care about gets hurt by others. It also means giving a little of yourself away and making yourself vulnerable so that others see the real you.

Mostly Bs – The get-involved friend/Follower friend You are a friend who is always willing to get involved, whether it's helping others out when they are down or gossiping for a laugh. People know you as the person everyone calls when things go pear shaped. However, be careful that you're doing all these things for the right reasons. Sometimes being overly helpful and there for friends is a way to avoid your own needs. It's also a way to protect yourself from being on the outside by making yourself invaluable to others. Don't be afraid to show people your other side (the angry, don't want to help side). Remember, real friends will love you warts and all.

Mostly Cs – The leader/Queen bee/Drama queen friend Whether you're a queen bee or not, you're a force to be reckoned with on the friendship front. Outspoken, forthright and often brutal with your delivery of advice, people tend to both admire and be afraid of you. This is good on the one hand as others won't mess with you or treat you badly, but it also means that you may be surrounded by followers who are too afraid to be your real friends. Consider softening up a bit – what harm could it do? Others don't need to do things to your standards to be your friend. Give them and yourself a break.

The problems of being a follower

"I know I'm a follower. I'm too afraid not to be. Sometimes my friends say stuff I don't agree with and I try not to do the stuff that's mean like throw dirty looks, but sometimes I have to. It's part of being friends and I like being with the popular girls."

CASEY, 13

Being a follower in a clique or with a queen bee or drama queen is tough. Aside from having to be at the beck-and-call of someone else all the time, it can be a scary place to be. Scary because you have to do what someone else wants for fear of getting on the wrong side of them! Scary because you often end up behaving in a way you know isn't right for you, and scary because you are too afraid to stop being friends with them in case you become the one who is excluded.

Followers also have to be what their name implies: not willing to challenge the leader for the spotlight. This means keeping the true you hidden, not disagreeing, not giving opinions and not being yourself.

At first being accepted into a clique, or by a queen bee, can be flattering and you don't mind doing the above. But eventually it becomes so second nature that you forget that you are allowed to have feelings and opinions too. Plus, whether you're doing the nasty tricks or not you are associated with them by others around you, which is bad news for your life outside of the clique and possibly another reason why you stay in with them.

What's more, in many cases followers are treated badly. The girls with the power in a clique can yo-yo with their like/dislike of you, put you down or maybe they subtly let you know that somehow you're not as good as the rest of them. As a result, followers tend to be people pleasers desperate to make everyone happy because they feel so insecure about their own status.

One way to break free of being a follower is to consider the impact it has on others and yourself. Cliques, and queen bees of the mean kind, only get to have their will enforced because they have followers (alone they just look like a bully). Likewise with drama queens and gossip girls, without followers to soak up the stress or pass on the rumours, they cannot achieve their goals.

So if you're a follower, ask yourself what you are getting from being part of the clique. Positives are likely to be: acceptance with the 'cool' girls, friendship of sorts and someone to hang out with. However, if fear is keeping you there or you're afraid of not being in the clique, then it's time to change your friendship style (see Chapter 5 for how to do this).

The problems of being a queen bee

"Yes, I am popular but it doesn't mean I am horrible. The thing is I don't have to be nice and be friends with everyone. Where does it say that?"

LEI, 12

At this point we have to say that not all queen bees are horrible and mean and treat people badly. However, many do. **The problem with being popular is that it gives you power.** Power to always get your way, power to pick and choose who you are friends with and power to get away with being mean and playing nasty tricks.

You're a queen bee if:

* *You get your friends to do what you want.*

* *You don't think there is anything wrong with ignoring or excluding other girls.*

* *You don't feel bad if you hurt other people's feelings.*

* *You seek revenge if you think someone has wronged you.*

* *You're good at hiding your actions from parents and teachers.*

The problem with being a queen bee is that 99% of the time you feel your actions, no matter how bad (whispering, dirty looks, excluding other girls), are justified. In your mind you believe you tried your best, but somehow this other girl let you down, didn't listen, or basically went against what you were saying. And that is at the heart of all your actions. It's your way or the highway!

However, being the queen bee is a lonely place to be because you're so busy maintaining your image (and the loyalty of your followers) that you can't let worries and fears surface. What's more, you can't afford to let others know when you feel sad or hurt, so in many ways you don't really feel you have true friendships that are based on actually liking each other.

If you're sick of being queen bee, you can change your friendship style right away by loosening the grip on your friends. You don't have to control people to be friends with them, but to let go you have to manage your emotions. This means keeping your jealousy at bay, redirecting your anger and not lashing out when a friend does something you don't like. There are many reformed queen bees who can tell you it doesn't take much to go from being popular and feared to being popular and liked.

The problems of being a gossip girl

"Everyone gossips and has dramas — they are lying if they don't. It makes school more exciting for a start and gives us all something to talk about."

LILY, 13

Knowing what's going on and why is another kind of power that friends can hold over each other. If you're a gossip girl or friends with one, you'll know how much knowing information about others can make a girl popular. In most cases the gossip girl is someone who likes to cause a stir or trouble by saying, 'X said this about Y', or, 'X kissed Y', or some other kind of salacious bit of info that's guaranteed to speed its way around everyone.

The power of social media has made the gossip girl's actions even more immediate, ensuring that whatever she says not only gets sent to everyone but also gets repeated and maybe even said anonymously (gossip girls nearly always deny they started a rumour). If you're a gossip girl, it's likely that you're good at befriending a lot of different people and great at appearing to keep secrets. You're also probably very smart at how you spread the gossip and have a good way of keeping under the radar and so you are rarely confronted about your actions.

The downside of your behaviour is that people don't trust you and so keep their distance. Can you honestly say you have close friends who trust you? Can you count on friends to be there for you when you need them? And what do you do when the gossip being spread is about you? That's why it's worth changing your ways. Betraying confidences not only hurts others (whether that was your intention or not) but also harms your reputation. Eventually people will work out that you're the source of the gossip/trouble and then the tables will turn.

The problems of being a drama queen

 "I am just a very sensitive person. Things upset me a lot and I need friends to lean on." **ALISON, 12**

Some people just have so much drama in their life. Whether it's exams, family problems or even a broken nail, each incident is blown into a full-scale emotional meltdown. If you're a drama queen it's likely that you do it for a variety of reasons:

* *Attention – having a meltdown is a guaranteed way to have people come running and look after you.*

* *Boredom – creating drama makes you feel that something interesting is happening in your life.*

* *Manipulation – your dramas are a way of keeping friends in your life and attached to you.*

The problem is, being a drama queen may be fun to you but it's exhausting (and irritating) for others and a sure way to eventually lose friends and people's respect. No one wants to be friends with someone who is (1) all about themselves and (2) energy draining. Yes, it's unfair that the maths teacher made you stand up and answer questions, but no one needs to hear it over and over. If you're keen to change your friendship behavior, you have to start by putting the brakes on your overreactions.

The way to do this is to practise keeping things in perspective. Things are rarely the end of the world, even if they feel like it. Not finding the shoes you want or having a boy you fancy ask you out may feel earth shattering but they're not. Remind yourself that you'll get over it and that you can handle it both rationally and calmly. Steer clear of saying things like, 'Why does this always happen to me?' Aside from being untrue, it just makes you think that drama follows you around.

Be aware of why you're reliving the dramas. It's not because you want a solution (drama queens rarely ask for or accept advice) but because you're addicted to the high of being the centre of attention. The good news is, as a drama queen you are naturally charismatic and able to get others to laugh. Use this side of you to entertain yourself and your friends. Remember, most people prefer a good comedy to a heartfelt drama any day.

Be aware of the impact that your dramatic behaviour has on others. Constant drama gives the impression to others that you are the only one who is important. If you're horrified by that thought, then you need to do all of the above right away. If, however, you believe that you are the most important, you need to think about why you feel that others should always put you first.

The problem with being different

 *"I just feel like I'm on the outside all the time. I don't get picked on but I am ignored. It's like I don't exist at school. No one wants to be my friend and no one likes the things I do. I hate school."*

SAMI, 12

Of course, we don't all fall into the above categories. Sometimes we can be the girl who used to be popular and now isn't, or the outsider who doesn't want to be popular and doesn't care about it. Or we can be the person who feels different and disconnected from others and someone who others are always picking on or simply ignoring.

If you feel like the girl who is different (for whatever reason) the good news is that studies show you're likely to do well in life. However, in the here and now it can feel tough. It could mean that you yearn for connection but can't see it in the cliques and girls that rule. Take heart, many people feel this way (though many hide it well). This is because it's hard to be different from others during a time when everyone wants to be the same, and so lots of people choose to fit in instead by hiding their true self.

In reality there are many people at school and in life who don't show their true colours for whatever reason. Just because someone doesn't look like a person you can be friends with, it doesn't mean that they are not for you. If you're struggling to fit in, it can help to pick one or two possible friends (choose the ones who smile at you and are nice) to focus on. Don't try too hard but be yourself, otherwise you can end up being friends for the wrong reasons and feeling even more disconnected.

Above all, remember you don't have to be a part of a group or follow someone to fit in. You can actually be friends with lots of different people and still refuse to be drawn into their conflicts.

If you're being targeted because you're an outsider or because you are different in some way, bear in mind that some queen bees feel challenged by those who dress differently, think differently and act differently. The answer here is not to tolerate it. Either reason with the people targeting you or seek help (see Help section on page 92 for more information). Remember, queen bees and cliques often pick on someone who is not connected to others because they know this is easier than going up against another group.

CHAPTER FIVE

When things go wrong

"Everything's gone wrong. Now I'm the one they make fun of and laugh at. They say I walk funny and that I kissed this boy behind his girlfriend's back. They are even getting me in trouble with the teachers."

ANON, 10

Inevitably in the friendship game, things can go horribly wrong. Sometimes you can be close and happy with your friends, only to turn up the next day and find yourself alienated and alone. Other times you can fall out over something trivial, and suddenly find yourself excluded from everyone. Then there are long-standing friendships that end or friends that continuously blow hot and cold on you. This sadly is all part of the friendship game and pretty unavoidable if you want to be close to others. It can be incredibly painful and frustrating and sometimes so distressing that it can upset your whole life.

What's important here is not to ignore it or pretend that it hasn't happened, but to learn how to handle these painful experiences.

Key points to remember are;

1) *Not every fall out marks the end of a friendship.*

2) *Not every friendship is made to last!*

The first thing you need to know is that friendships are nearly always volatile, partly because these relationships are so close. When someone knows you inside and out, spends all her time with you and feels that you get them, it's a wonderful and happy experience. However, as in any close relationship this also means that irritations arise easily and people get sensitive, jealous, angry and hurt, especially when you're friends with others too. This then leads to all kinds of behaviours that  go against the very nature of being friends.

For instance, you might find yourself experiencing things such as being rejected and excluded or being ignored and being talked about behind your back. Teachers and parents may tell you to make up, move on or simply to ignore it, but it can be hard to do any of those things when you feel hurt and rejected. We all know that we shouldn't forgive friends who treat us badly, or try to please those who are putting us down, but sometimes this can feel like the only option.

Handling cliques who turn on you

"It's horrible when your friends stop being friends with you. They just stare you out all the time and make it clear you're a loser."

ANNA, 13

Cliques, as we have said before, are powerful machines ruled by one person and backed up by others. If they turn on you it can feel like the most terrifying thing in the world. Aside from being painful, it can feel as if you have no one to turn to. When it happens ask yourself the following:

What's behind this? Has something concrete happened? Did you disagree, express an opinion or hurt someone intentionally or not? Are they jealous in some way? Can you pinpoint why they are turning on you?

Has the clique acted like this before towards someone and why? Thinking back to past events and conflicts with other girls can give you an idea as to why a clique has turned on you. Is their behaviour usually based on something petty, or real, or is it a power play?

How do you feel about what's happening? Aside from being hurt and afraid, are you angry or maybe fed up? This tends to indicate that you've had enough of the behaviour of the clique and you want to be rid of them.

What do you want to happen next? Really think about this question, as it will give you a direction to go in. Your immediate answer may be that you want them to take you back and this to all be forgotten, BUT don't forget how they've made you feel. Do you really want to be friends with people like this? Wouldn't you rather feel on safer ground?

What are you going to do? Deciding what you're going to do gives you back the control and takes away that helpless feeling. Think strategy – do you want to make amends? Would this make them respect you again? Do you want to break away, in which case is this a good excuse to back off? Or do you want to calm the waters, so you don't feel always on edge, and then back away? Only you can decide, though bear in mind that it's always better to choose a tactic that you have control over rather than trying to make up and being rejected. Ask if they want to talk about it. If they are mean or just laugh or refuse, take it as a sign that you should not be in this clique any more.

Handling queen bees

"She hates me and never misses a chance to make my life miserable."

ROS, 11

Going up against a queen bee is frightening. Queen bees can be aggressive about maintaining what they have and vicious to those who try to stand up to them. Don't get angry or tearful when confronting a queen bee, but think strategy. Firstly you need to think about what's happening – is it teasing or taunting and bullying?

Teasing is good-natured humour that isn't done to hurt or belittle you. People who tease stop and apologize when you tell them they have hurt your feelings and teasing doesn't have an agenda behind it.

Taunting and bullying, on the other hand, always has an agenda, whether it's to hurt you, assert power, or get revenge (usually over some slight offense you'll never even know about). It tends to be purposefully hurtful, done in groups and continuous over days and weeks. When confronted, it is denied or the blame is cast on you.

Queen bees exclude by:

* *Turning friends against you.*

* *Letting it be known that they don't like you any more.*

* *Teasing and taunting.*

* *Name-calling, dirty looks, whispering and laughter.*

* *Attacking your family or looks.*

* *Mimicking you.*

If the above is happening to you, **write it down.** Record everything that happens to you and when. This not only helps you to be clear about it in your mind, but also gives you something to fall back on if you need to take it further (as in take it to your parents and the teachers). If you are going to confront the queen bee, this can also help you to get the facts clear in your mind. If your strategy is to talk to the queen bee, always do it in person (texts, emails or Skype messages can be copied and sent round to everyone), and be sure to do it away from her followers so she doesn't feel as if she has to put on a show or lose face.

Be very clear about what you want to happen in a confrontation. Are you looking for an apology, to make up or for the mean behaviours to stop? Or are you appealing to her to stop getting at you?

Knowing how the queen bee is likely to respond will give you your answer. If she is adept at being two-faced, then you can't trust what she says and does in a confrontation. If she never accepts blame, then she's likely to blame one of her followers and pretend that it's nothing to do with her (don't be fooled).

If she hates being cornered, she's likely to get aggressive (if she's known for getting physical do not confront her). She may also either blame you or say she doesn't know why you're picking on her! If by any chance your words do get through, then the best you can expect is to feel you have achieved your goal and she will leave you alone. Do not expect to make up and be friends, because she won't do this, and really, do you want to be friends with her?

The queen bee confrontation checklist:

* *Talk to her alone, away from everyone.*

* *Be sure you're safe with her (do not confront her if she is overly aggressive).*

* *Know what you want to say. Be clear and concise and have between one and three clear points. Eg. I don't like your doing X, Y and Z, please stop.*

* *Know your outcome (for the behaviour to stop/for an apology/to be friends again).*

* *Prepare for her to deny knowledge or blame others.*

* *Stick to your points.*

* *Do not ask why she's doing it as you're unlikely to hear the truth and this just gives her an opportunity to blame you.*

* *Tell her you will take it further if she doesn't stop.*

Being excluded, ignored and rejected by friends

"They used to be my friends. Now they just walk away every time I come near them."

T.K., 10

Sometimes you can try everything and you still feel as if you don't fit in, or that people don't like you any more. Maybe they don't get your sense of humour, they don't like the music you're into or they simply can't be bothered to be friends any more. But that doesn't mean you have to try harder, or change who you are or even try to copy the people around you.

Being excluded can take many forms – from people refusing to sit next to you or looking away when you speak, to people talking over you, or not inviting you out (but letting you know they all went out).

Being ignored can mean not being asked to join in, being dismissed when you say something, being forgotten during team sports or not having a partner when you have to team up.

Being rejected tends to occur between girls that were once friends. It can be anything from having people move away from you in class or not sitting next to you in lunch, to seeing people whisper about you, or throw dirty looks your way.

Hard as it is, you have to stay true to yourself and ignore all the people who get you down. Speak up to the bullying aspects (if any), but sometimes you have to put up with being ignored, excluded and even rejected by others. The way to cope with this is to focus on the fact that you are a good person and worth knowing even if others can't see it. Having friends in the real world outside of school can help confirm this to you. There are plenty of people who aren't popular at school, but have many friends outside of school.

The benefit of having friends away from school is immense in terms of confidence, as it enables you to choose friends based on who you really are, not just because you're in the same class. Expand what you do and try to make friends outside of school. Join an after-school group for drama, or sports, volunteer or sign up to a website based on one of your hobbies and meet some like-minded people (though be wary of who you are talking to see Chatdanger in the Help section on page 92).

The key here is to prove to yourself that who you are at school isn't who you are in life. Though school feels like everything and its impact spreads across your life, it doesn't have to be the marker for how you feel about yourself. Once it's over, you'll realize that making friends in work and at college is way easier and much less complicated.

A word of warning though, being pushed away by people and friends is something you sometimes have to cope with and you MUST talk about the emotional side of this to someone. Whether it's someone you know or a helpline, talking will help you to understand your feelings.

Don't suffer in silence. When we hide the things that hurt us they tend to eat us up inside, making us feel as if there is something wrong with us, and that we don't deserve things. If this goes on long enough, it can lead to serious feelings of depression and worse. The trick to coping (and that's coping with anything in life) is to tell someone you trust how you feel and let him or her help you feel better.

If you're being excluded and rejected:

DO *Let others know what's happening to you.*

DON'T *Try to please people who are mean to you.*

DO *Remember that you haven't done anything wrong.*

DON'T *Blame yourself.*

DO *Look for new friends around the school and in your class.*

DON'T *Run after those who are rejecting you.*

DO *Take it as a sign that these people weren't your true friends.*

DON'T *Imagine that everyone thinks of you in this way.*

DO *Remember that one day you'll have lots of friends better than these people.*

Breaking away from drama queens

"I feel too guilty to stop being her friend. She needs me."

RHIAN, 10

Rest assured, that there is never ever a good time to break away from a drama queen. This is because not a day goes by when there isn't some drama causing the drama queen some kind of misery. However, you know you have had enough when you feel totally drained and can't bear the thought of another meltdown from her.

The best way to break away from a drama queen is to slowly detach yourself from her. A sudden break will cause a massive emotional response. If you feel the friendship is salvageable, then what you need to do is talk to her about being less needy. Also be aware that often drama queens get away with their dramatics because their friends unwittingly encourage them. If you're always rushing to her aid, sympathizing with her, extending the drama by asking how she is or telling others what's wrong with her, then you need to pull back. By all means offer sympathy, but limit it and move on.

Try saying:

* *'Oh no that's really bad but let's do X to make you feel better.'*

* *'I'm sorry to hear that, but did you hear that X and Y happened today?'*

* *'Oh no, but maybe X would help as it did last time.'*

Above all avoid being pulled into a massive discussion about the event in question. Often drama queens try to extend their dramas by making them dilemmas that cannot be solved. The drama queen will ask for advice but really she doesn't want any advice from you – she just wants to wallow in her drama with your aid.

Detach by:

* Not letting her call/text/message you at all hours.

* Not being drawn into the dramas.

* Not over-sympathizing.

* Reaching out to other friends or new friends.

* Thinking about what you're getting from this friendship.

* Bringing yourself into the conversation.

Best friend break ups

"We used to be best friends but since last summer we haven't spoken. It's sad but I'm also angry about it."

LEANNE, 12

One of the first rules of friendship is to realize that no matter how close you are, not all friendships are made to last. Just like dating, friendships tend to come and go, especially in your teens when you radically change your likes and dislikes and start to become a new, more grown-up person. As this rite of passage happens at a different rate for everyone (it's linked to puberty in case you were wondering), you'll find that friendships start to crumble and break up. Even if you don't want them to, you might find yourself suddenly having nothing in common with a friend you used to laugh with all the time. Or becoming irritated and annoyed with a friend who you are very close to. You may also find yourself being drawn towards new friends and groups, while your old friend lags behind.

If you're the friend moving on, remember to be kind about it. It's never nice to feel rejected or left behind and you can help by maintaining a kind of friendship with your old friend (old friends are worth their weight in gold, especially when you're older and looking back). Of course, they may not take the change well but you can help the transition by:

* *Reassuring them that you're still friends.*

* *Not making them feel rejected or jealous of your new friends.*

* *Spending some time together.*

* *Being careful not to rub their faces in the fact that you have new friends.*

* *Encouraging them to try out new things and new friends.*

* *Being sensitive to the fact that they will be hurt by you moving on.*

If you're on the other side of it and being left behind, as painful as it is try to see it as a new start. Sometimes, having to find new friends can open up a whole new lease of life for you. It can help you to see that you're more than you think you are, and help you to develop into the person you want to be. New friends can literally be found everywhere – from girls you haven't taken notice of in class (being best friends with someone often cuts you off from other potential friends because you're so wrapped up in each other), to people you meet out of school

or online (though again be wary of the dangers of meeting friends online – see Help section for more on this).

Help yourself by not:

* ❋ *Clinging on to friendships that have changed.*
* ❋ *Blaming yourself for a friend leaving.*
* ❋ *Changing who you are to please others.*
* ❋ *Thinking there is something wrong with you.*
* ❋ *Wanting revenge for the rejection.*
* ❋ *Bad mouthing your ex-friend.*

A word about yo-yo friends

"One minute she's my best friend, the next she is ignoring me. I am always wondering what I have done to annoy her or upset her. What do I do?"

CLARE, 12

While we've gone through the main categories of friends, you may also come across one of the lesser-known species – the yo-yo friend. **Yo-yo friends are the friends that blow hot and cold on you.** One minute they are your best friend – and can't do enough for you – but the next they are ignoring you and throwing dirty looks. Then just when you've had enough they are back again, begging to be friends. The problem with having a yo-yo friend is that it puts you on a rollercoaster of emotions where you never really know where you stand. Plus it makes you feel alternately grateful for the attention and guilty and rejected for losing it. Not a good place to be.

You have a yo-yo friend if:

* *You feel as if you're walking on eggshells with them.*

* *You are always worried they will turn on you.*

* *When they turn, they are nasty.*

* *When they're nice, you feel grateful.*

* *You keep thinking they will change.*

The best way to deal with a yo-yo friend is to acknowledge that they do it both for thrills and the power it gives them. Knowing that they have full power over who they are and aren't friends with gives them a thrill. They also focus on the short-term benefits so when they are happy with you they really do want to be your best friend, but when they're with someone else they're focused on that. The problem is, sticking around with a yo-yo friend is bad news for you because it gives her the message that she can do what she likes and you will still be there for her. Friends who genuinely like you and care about you don't rattle your emotions like this.

Making up or breaking up

"She says she's sorry for what she did but I don't know whether to trust her or not. She was so mean to me, excluding me from her party, turning friends against me and making me cry. Now she says she's sorry for losing me, that she was wrong, but I don't feel I can trust her again. What do I do?"

ANON, 11

Ultimately when you fight with friends, only you can say if it's worth making up or breaking up. Sometimes a friendship will be worth sticking with and other times it's clearly time to call it a day. The key here is the balance between what you have as friends and what's happened in your fall out. If the argument has been a small one that's been blown out of proportion, it will be fairly easy to get your trust levels back with a bit of work. However, if it's been major and there has been a lot of hurt and anxiety, becoming friends again can be difficult.

This is because friendships are based on trust and when that's gone, so too is a friendship. If you're stuck about what to do, consider this: Does being friends with them make you more happy than unhappy? The answer to this is the answer to whether or not you should remain friends.

Break up if this person:

* *Makes you feel unworthy.*

* *Has made your life a misery.*

* *Never says sorry.*

* *Takes pleasure in upsetting others.*
* *Is only interested in herself.*

Stay friends if this person:

* *Really makes you feel good about who you are.*
* *Makes you laugh more than cry.*
* *Has your best interests at heart.*
* *Says sorry when she hurts you.*
* *Is a good friend who cares about others.*

8 ways to empower yourself against hurtful friends

For most of this book we've spoken about the ways to improve your friendships, deal with friendships that are bad and improve your own friendship behaviours. To handle all of the above, one of the most important things to do is empower yourself with confidence so that you don't fall to pieces when friendships go wrong.

The key aspect here is self-esteem – improving the way you feel about yourself. When you feel good about who you are, you are more likely to choose good friends, not put up with dirty tricks, and not be crushed when friends leave you.

Of course, this is easier said than done when inside you feel unworthy, or not good enough, pretty enough or smart enough. It can be very hard to do when everyone around you is doing their very best to trample on your self-esteem. The good news is it can be done by changing the way you speak to yourself, challenging those who put you down (in your head rather than in person if you don't feel up to it), and reinforcing what you know about yourself.

If you're keen to empower yourself here are eight ways to do it...

1 Improve how you speak to yourself. Silencing that negative voice inside your head is the number one way to improve your self-esteem. Every time you hear the voice saying something like, 'You're horrible, that's why no one wants to be your friend' – silence it by challenging what you're saying to yourself. For example, if friends ignore you:

Your voice says: 'You deserve that. You did something wrong.'
You challenge it by saying: 'No I didn't.'

Your voice says: 'Yes, but you're lucky to have them. No one else wants to be friends with you.'
You say: 'That's not true (and give yourself examples).'

Your voice says: 'But you must have done something wrong?'
You say: 'No, they are doing something wrong.'

If you consistently speak nicely to yourself you'll feel better about yourself, and you will start to demand that others treat you with respect too. This in turn will make others less likely to put you down.

2 Get a life away from school. Not everyone is made to love school. Many people cannot wait to get away from the petty squabbles, mean girls and nasty tricks. However, you do have to go to school so this means making it more bearable. One way to do this is to make sure you have a fun and happy life away from school. Join clubs and groups away from school and make friends from scratch. Being friends with others based on your interests, rather than the fact you're in the same class, is a massive self-esteem booster.

3 Learn to say less. Do not give your friends and the girls you know ammunition by telling them too much about your private life. Yes, you may trust your friends, but do you really want to tell them something incredibly personal that may get out one day? Likewise, be careful what you say and post on social media sites – something fun may turn into something you're teased about, and something said in innocence can be turned against you. If you're unsure whether to post it or send it, this is a sign that you probably shouldn't.

4 Get sporty and active. Feeling stronger physically is a guaranteed way to feel stronger mentally. Getting fit also improves your body image and the way you feel about yourself. Getting sporty doesn't mean being brilliant at PE, or one sport – it simply means getting more active, going out and doing things that make you feel healthy, whether it's biking, walking, dancing or all them! Exercise releases endorphins – these are feel-good chemicals that make you feel as if you can take on anything.

5 Be true to yourself. This one is hard, especially when you're surrounded by peer pressure. The compromise to make is to stay true to yourself inside but let the more flaky things slide. So keep to your morals and what you believe is right and wrong (this is especially relevant in your actions to other girls and what you accept and don't accept), but if you feel you have to have your hair a certain way to fit in then go for it. If you don't know who you are on the inside, have a think about what you believe is right and wrong. Should one girl be able to make everyone unhappy? What is the definition of being a true friend? Do you have to think like everyone else to fit in? What core beliefs make up who you are?

6 Don't compare yourself to others. Comparing yourself to others is just putting yourself down. There will always be people who are prettier, smarter and more popular than you (in the same way that there will be people less pretty, less smart and less popular than you). Is this something to get down about and punish yourself with? No it's not, it's life and you have to learn to deal with it. What's important is not what someone else does or looks like, but what you do and how you feel about yourself.

7 Realize that not everyone is made to be queen bee. You may wish you were the most popular girl at school, but not everyone can be queen bee (and thank goodness for that). While you may not ever be the most popular girl at school, there's nothing to stop you being super popular to the friends and family that matter. Don't waste your time wishing that you were something you're not. Make the most of your own skills and gifts, and you'll not only be happier but you'll also be too busy to care about what others are doing.

8 Don't isolate yourself when you're upset. The worst thing you can do when you're feeling down or picked on by friends is to isolate yourself and keep quiet about it. Bullies know that it's a feeling of shame that keeps their victims quiet. A sense that you have let it happen and that other people may be disappointed in you because it's happening. This couldn't be further from the truth. Isolating yourself intensifies this feeling of being to blame, whereas telling others releases it and stops you feeling helpless and alone. Keep the lines of communication open at home and with the people who care about you. It may feel as if your friends are your whole world, but the good news is, they aren't!

Help section

These organizations' websites have more help and advice if you are having problems with friends or are being bullied. Many of the websites have contact details if you need to talk to someone or have questions.

Being a girl
http://www.beinggirl.co.uk/
A good advice site looking at health and friendships.

Bullying at school
https://www.gov.uk/bullying-at-school
Information on the law and how to report bullying.

Bullying UK
http://www.bullying.co.uk/ 0808 800 2222
You can email, chat live or Skype a counsellor.

Campaign for body confidence
http://campaignforbodyconfidence.wordpress.com/
Boosting self-esteem and confidence.

Chatdanger
http://www.chatdanger.com/
Advice and help on how to keep safe while chatting online. Includes everything from online abuse to keeping safe on mobiles, texts, IM, emails and online games.

ChildLine
http://www.childline.org.uk/ 0800 1111
For help and advice on a wide range of issues. You can talk to a confidential counsellor online by sending ChildLine an email or by posting on the message boards.

Family lives
http://familylives.org.uk/ 0808 800 2222
Help and advice for parents, on all issues relating to teen friendships, bullying and online harassment.

Give yourself a chance
http://www.girlguiding.org.uk/news/self-esteem_tips_for_girls.aspx
A site designed to offer tips to young women and ways to boost self-esteem.

Kidscape
http://www.kidscape.org.uk/
Advice and help on everything from bullying to making friends and online problems.

Quib.ly
http://quib.ly
Provides information and advice on a range of social networking, tech and social media questions.

TheSite
http://www.thesite.org/
An online guide to life for older teens aged 16–25. Support is available 24 hours a day. Chat about any issue on moderated discussion boards and in a live chat room, browse over 2,000 articles and videos by professional journalists, or ask a question and get an answer within three working days.

* The website addresses (URLs) included in this book were valid at the time of going to press. However, because of the nature of the Internet, it is possible that some addresses may have changed, or sites may have changed or closed down since publication. While the authors and publishers regret any inconvenience this may cause the readers, no responsibility for any such changes can be accepted by either the authors or the publisher.

Glossary

Clique – an exclusive group of friends who do not let others into their friendship group.

Confrontation – standing up to or facing up to someone.

Cyberbullying – using electronic communication and technology to bully a person; for example by sending threatening or unkind messages by text, via social media and other online platforms.

Drama queen – a girl who uses emotional behaviour to control her friends.

Exclusion – this can take many forms, from people refusing to sit next to you, to people looking away when you speak, people talking over you or people not inviting you out (but letting you know they all went out).

Followers – people who follow a queen bee/popular girl and do her bidding.

Gossip – rumours, half-truths, secrets and made-up information that get spread between friends.

Insidious – seemingly harmless repetitive actions that can be very harmful and distressing.

Instant messaging (IM) – real-time communication between a group via an App or social network.

Manipulation – controlling or influencing someone to behave in a certain way (good or bad).

Popular – liked/followed by many people.

Psychological games – mind games that affect the way you think about yourself and others.

Queen bee – a girl who is in charge of a group of friends, usually a clique.

Relational aggression – the use of friendship as a weapon where girls gain power and attention and respect from others, even those who don't like them, through a variety of methods such as excluding others.

Role model – a person you admire (for looks, skills, talents or something else) that you model yourself on.

Self-esteem – how you feel about yourself. High self-esteem means liking yourself, low self-esteem means disliking yourself.

Tagged – to be identified in a picture or video (so everyone following you can see it too).

Index